TOOLS FOR CAREGIVERS

- **F&P LEVEL:** C
- **WORD COUNT:** 32

- **CURRICULUM CONNECTIONS:** holidays, traditions

Skills to Teach

- **HIGH-FREQUENCY WORDS:** a, get, is, it, see, we
- **CONTENT WORDS:** eat, envelopes, family, fireworks, hang, inside, lanterns, lunar, money, new, parade, red, wear, year
- **PUNCTUATION:** exclamation points, periods
- **WORD STUDY:** compound words (*fireworks*, *inside*); long /e/, spelled *ea* (*eat*, *year*); long /e/, spelled *y* (*family*); /oo/, spelled *ew* (*new*)
- **TEXT TYPE:** information report

Before Reading Activities

- Read the title and give a simple statement of the main idea.
- Have students "walk" through the book and talk about what they see in the pictures.
- Introduce new vocabulary by having students predict the first letter and locate the word in the text.
- Discuss any unfamiliar concepts that are in the text.

After Reading Activities

Flip through the book again with readers. What do they see? How are people in the book celebrating Lunar New Year? Have each reader draw their favorite Lunar New Year tradition and share it with the group.

Tadpole Books are published by Jump!, 5357 Penn Avenue South, Minneapolis, MN 55419, www.jumplibrary.com

Copyright ©2025 Jump. International copyright reserved in all countries. No part of this book may be reproduced in any form without written permission from the publisher.

Editor: Alyssa Sorenson   **Designer:** Molly Ballanger

Photo Credits: Runrun2/Shutterstock, cover; dezign56/Shutterstock, 1, 11; Makistock/Shutterstock, 2tl, 10; Dragon Images/Shutterstock, 2tr, 3, 16; lusea/iStock, 2ml, 14–15; Drazen Zigic/iStock, 2mr, 4–5; Steve Sanchez Photos/Shutterstock, 2bl, 12–13; 1981 Rustic Studio kan/Shutterstock, 2br, 6; TuTheLens/iStock, 7; Koh Sze Kiat/iStock, 8–9.

Library of Congress Cataloging-in-Publication Data
Names: Austen, Lily, author.
Title: Lunar New Year / by Lily Austen.
Description: Minneapolis, MN: Jump!, Inc., [2025]
Series: Holiday fun! | Includes index.
Audience: Ages 3–6
Identifiers: LCCN 2024019859 (print)
LCCN 2024019860 (ebook)
ISBN 9798892135047 (hardcover)
ISBN 9798892135054 (paperback)
ISBN 9798892135061 (ebook)
Subjects: LCSH: New Year—Juvenile literature.
Classification: LCC GT4905 .A97 2025 (print)
LCC GT4905 (ebook)
DDC 394.2614—dc23/eng/20240501
LC record available at https://lccn.loc.gov/2024019859
LC ebook record available at https://lccn.loc.gov/2024019860

HOLIDAY FUN!

LUNAR NEW YEAR

by Lily Austen

TABLE OF CONTENTS

Words to Know	2
Lunar New Year	3
Let's Review!	16
Index	16

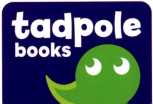

WORDS TO KNOW

envelopes

family

fireworks

lanterns

parade

wear

We wear red.

We see family.

Money is inside.

We see a parade.

We see fireworks!

LET'S REVIEW!

Lunar New Year celebrates the new year and spring. How is this family celebrating?

INDEX

envelopes 10
family 8
fireworks 15
lanterns 5
parade 13
red 7